Police Lieutenant Exam

Police Lieutenant Exam #1

Test Taking Tips

☐ Take a deep breath and relax

☐ Read directions carefully

☐ Read the questions thoroughly

☐ Make sure you understand what is being asked

☐ Go over all of the choices before you answer

☐ Paraphrase the question

☐ Eliminate the options you know are wrong

☐ Check your work

☐ Think positively and do your best

Table of Contents

TEST DIRECTION

DIRECTIONS

Read the questions carefully and then choose the ONE best answer to each question.

Be sure to allocate your time carefully so you are able to complete the entire test within the testing session. You may go back and review your answers at any time.

You may use any available space in your test booklet for scratch work.

Questions in this booklet are not actual test questions but they are the samples for commonly asked questions.

This test aims to cover all topics which may appear on the actual test. However some topics may not be covered.

Studying this booklet will be preparing you for the actual test. It will not guarantee improving your test score but it will help you pass your exam on the first attempt.

Some useful tips for answering multiple choice questions;

- Start with the questions that you can easily answer.

- Underline the keywords in the question.

- Be sure to read all the choices given.

- Watch for keywords such as NOT, always, only, all, never, completely.

- Do not forget to answer every question.

1

"I've watched the ocean lashed by wind,"

In this line from the poem, "I've Watched…" which of the following does the underlined word mean?

A) sailed
B) troubled
C) whipped
D) soothed

2

You are given the following sentence. From the options below pick the most suitable words to accurately complete the sentence.

Joanna never drinks … because she thinks it tastes … .

A) juice; delicious
B) soda; amazing
C) coffee; bitter
D) milk; wonderful

3

"5 feet 11 inches is the height of the shortest member of the basketball team. Jaron is 6 feet 2 inches tall."

Which of the following is a fact when considering the passage above?

A) Jaron is shorter than some members of the basketball team.
B) At least one member of the basketball team is shorter than Jaron.
C) Only members of the basketball team are taller than 5 feet 11 inches.
D) Jaron is the tallest member of the basketball team.

4

According to the preceding paragraph when can an employee be considered an accident-prone prone?

A) When he/she has accidents regardless of the fact that he/she had undergone a proper training.
B) When he/she has many accident cases.
C) When he/she has a possibility to be involved in accidents.
D) When his/her job poses possible accidents.

5

"Please allow at least four weeks for diagnosing the problem and repairing the radio."

In the passage which of the does "diagnosing" mean?

A) It means to identify.
B) It means to read about.
C) It means asking about.
D) It means to restored.

6

You are given the following sentence. From the options below pick the most suitable words to accurately complete the sentence.

… animals have to live in … cages.

A) good; huge
B) small; new
C) large; big
D) small; new

7

You are given the following sentence. From the options below pick the most suitable words to accurately complete the sentence.

Although the house may appear … from the outside, Cathy assures me that the interior is quite … .

A) bright; colorful
B) expensive; large
C) plain; fancy
D) small; tiny

8

You are given the following sentence. From the options below pick the most suitable words to accurately complete the sentence.

It takes … hands to hit a target with a bow and arrow.

A) agile
B) rough
C) steady
D) delicate

9

Capitalization is the action of writing or printing in capital letters or with an initial capital. Which of the below lines follows these rules?

A) Dr. Abby griffin
B) appointed as The
C) new director of current affairs
D) january 2, 2014

10

You are given the following sentence. From the options below pick the most suitable words to accurately complete the sentence.

Joanna never drinks … because she thinks it tastes … .

A) juice; delicious
B) soda; amazing
C) coffee; bitter
D) milk; wonderful

11

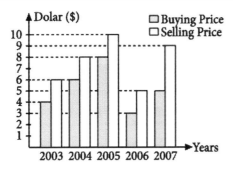

The column chart given above shows the buying and selling prices of items sold in a store between 2003 and 2007. How many percent is the profit margin of the store make a profit in 2007?

A) 40
B) 50
C) 80
D) 90

12

A	K	O	R	Z
1	2	3	4	5

Which of the following choices contains the letters add up to 9 after they are converted to numbers?

A) K,R,Z
B) O,A,R
C) O,R,Z
D) A,O,Z

13

You are given the following sentence. From the options below pick the most suitable words to accurately complete the sentence.

Lauren doesn't like to wear ... , so she wears ... instead.

A) makeup; paint
B) sweaters; jeans
C) shoes; mittens
D) skirts; pants

14

You are given the following sentence. From the options below pick the most suitable words to accurately complete the sentence.

Despite Maria's best efforts at making Melinda feel ... , she felt very ... at the party.

A) relaxed; uncomfortable
B) sociable; odd
C) helpful; generous
D) miserable; sad

What is the proper alphabetical order of the following names?

1. Maxwell, Alexander
2. Maxwell, Alexandra
3. Maxwell, Alexandro
4. Maxwell, Alexandre

A) 1,2,3,4
B) 2,3,1,4
C) 1,4,2,3
D) 1,2,4,3

Given the following scenario, choose the best option from the list below.

Facts: For her birthday, Jenny receives a box with flavored chocolates. Some of the chocolates are strawberry flavored, half of the chocolates are caramel, and the chocolates which are neither of those are cherry flavored.

Conclusion: There are more strawberry flavored chocolates in the box than cherry flavored ones.

A) The facts neither prove nor disprove the conclusion.
B) The facts are in accordance with the conclusion.
C) The facts are not in accordance with the conclusion.
D) None of the above.

17

Read the following scenario and choose the best option from the list below.

Facts: During a game involving letters, Phillip writes down only words that start with consonants, while Jeremy writes down only words that start with vowels. At the same time, Robert writes down only words that start with the letter M.

Conclusion: Jeremy and Robert did not both write words starting with the same letter.

A) The facts neither prove nor disprove the conclusion.
B) The facts are not in accordance with the conclusion.
C) The facts are in in accordance with the conclusion.
D) None of the above.

18

Which of the following choices contains letters that would sum up to 17 after the respective letters are converted to numbers?

A) A,E,E,B,E,X
B) C,C,X,E,D
C) X,B,E,D,C
D) E,X,D,C,E

19

There are four cards parked side by side in a parking lot. The blue car is parked on the far left. The yellow car is immediately next to the red car. The green car is between the yellow and blue cars. Miriam's car is between the blue and red cars.

Based on the details described in the passage, which of the following sentences is true?

A) The green car is parked right next to the blue car.
B) The green car is positioned right next to the red car.
C) The color of Miriam's car is green.
D) The color of Miriam's car is yellow.

20

You are given the following scenario, choose the best option from the list below.

Facts: In a business accounting firm with ten floors, Melinda's office is located on the third floor of the building. Jason's office is two floors below Robert's, whose office is on the eight floor of the building.

Conclusion: Jason works in the upper half of the firm's building.

A) The facts neither prove nor disprove the conclusion.
B) The facts are in accordance with the conclusion.
C) The facts are not in accordance with the conclusion.
D) None of the above.

21

You are given the following sentence. From the options below pick the most suitable words to accurately complete the sentence.

Because of Chelsey's ... attitude, many were ... to trust her as leader of the science group.

A) apathetic; compelled
B) uncaring; reluctant
C) good; unwilling
D) negative; eager

22

"When Joo Hyuk listens to music, he also dances. Whenever he dances, he also sings."

What can you conclude based on the information given?

A) When Joo Hyuk listens to music, then he is also singing.
B) If Joo Hyuk is not listening to music, then he is not dancing.
C) Joo Hyuk only sings when he is dancing.
D) When Joo Hyuk sings, then he is dancing.

23

"I leaned against the rough brick exterior and daydreamed about what I'd rather be doing. "Almost anything," I sighed <u>dejectedly</u>. I had been tutored enough to read, understand, and even writ some musical compositions, but I just didn't have a flair for it."

What does the underlined word mean in the passage?

A) Unhappily
B) Quietly
C) Quickly
D) uncontrollably

You are given the following sentence. From the options below pick the most suitable words to accurately complete the sentence.

Unlike the ... hair of his dog, Leo's horse has ... hair, making it much easier to groom.

A) curly; straight
B) smooth; uneven
C) rough; black
D) thick; rough

Henry asked 20 students how many states, besides Louisiana, they had visited. The line plot below shows the results.

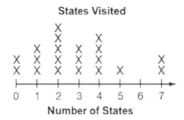

Which statement best describes the distribution of the data from Henry's survey?

A) Half of the students had visited 2 or more states.
B) Half of the students had visited exactly 2 states.
C) Half of the students had visited the same 2 states.
D) Half of the students had visited 2 or fewer states.

26

Given the following scenario, choose the best option from the list below.

Facts: Maria has $1 and $5 bills in her purse. The number of $5 bills is twice the number of $1 bills.

Conclusion: Maria has in her purse exact change for a $20 bill.

A) The facts neither prove nor disprove the conclusion.
B) The facts are in accordance with the conclusion.
C) The facts are not in accordance with the conclusion.
D) None of the above.

27

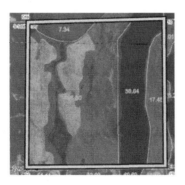

A parcel of property having an area of 2,356,000 square feet has a width of 3100 feet. How deep is the property?

A) 3100 Feet
B) 2350 Feet
C) 18.9%
D) 760 Feet

28

You are given the following sentence. From the options below pick the most suitable words to accurately complete the sentence.

The doctor takes note of any … blemishes on the patient's skin seeing as such abnormalities are often … of skin cancer.

A) small; indications
B) irregular; symptoms
C) common; causes
D) interesting; signs

29

You are given the following sentence. From the options below pick the most suitable words to accurately complete the sentence.

The new restaurant gets … reviews, so we have … eating there.

A) mediocre; recommended
B) pleasant; evaded
C) terrible; disliked
D) awful; avoided

30

A dozen of pencils is worth $2.50, a ream of bond paper is worth $9.50, and each box of paper clips is worth $.80. A court officer is requested to procure three dozens of pencil, two reams of bond paper, and three boxes of paper clips.

How much is the total cost?

A) $26.90
B) $18.90
C) $28.90
D) More than $30.00

31

A baseball coach places baseballs in a cart. He uses the baseballs to pitch to the players during practice. The number of baseballs remaining in the cart after different practice lengths, in minutes, are displayed in the scatter plot below.

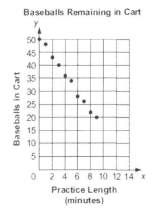

Which statement about the scatter plot is true?

A) The scatter plot shows a negative association because the practice length is always less than the number of baseballs in the cart.
B) The scatter plot shows a positive association because all of the points have positive coordinates.
C) The scatter plot shows a negative association because as the practice length increases, the number of baseballs in the cart decreases.
D) The scatter plot shows a positive association because the points on the graph go towards 50 baseballs.

CONTINUE ▶

32

"By mutual agreement, the first session was limited to domestic issues. Each candidate was given eight minutes to make his opening remarks. During the remainder of the hour, the candidates took turns responding to questions posed by selected reporters. Both Kennedy and Nixon dealt with the issues calmly and carefully."

Based on the passage above, which of the would be the possible concern to be disussed on the first session of debate between Kennedy and Nixon?

A) World nuclear disarmament
B) Trade with Europe
C) Problems of American industry
D) Politics of the Middle East

33

"The wild behavior and skills of the falcon are treasured by the falconer. The reward in working with a trained falcon is the companionship of a creature that can choose at any time to disappear over the horizon forever."

Which of the following does the phrase "disappear over the horizon" imply in the given passage?

A) Fly very high
B) Return to the falconer
C) Abandon the falconer
D) Go behind trees

34

Laundry Schedule

Time	Inmate Group	Duration
9:05 a.m.	Group K	35 minutes
9:45 a.m.	Group L	45 minutes
10:25 a.m.	Group M	40 minutes
11:30 a.m.	Group N	35 minutes
12:10 p.m.	Group O	55 minutes

The table above gives the laundry schedule for the day in a facillity. Which of the following two groups have library times that overlap with each other?

A) Group K and Group L
B) Group L and Group M
C) Group M and Group N
D) Group N and Group O

Ladder length	# of people to carry the ladder
10	2
20	3
30	4
40	5

Ladder size and number of people needed to carry the ladder is presented in the above table. Which of the following describes the relationship between the length of a ladder and the number of firefighter needed to carry that ladder?

A) As the ladder length is doubled, the number of people needed to carry it is also doubled

B) As the ladder length is tripled, the number of people needed to carry it is doubled.

C) The longer the ladder, the fewer the number of people needed to carry it.

D) There is a linear relationship between the length of ladder and the number of people needed to carry it.

A movie theater kept track of the attendance on Fridays and Saturdays. The results are shown in the box plots below.

Movie Theatre Attendance

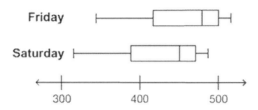

Which conclusion can be drawn from the box plots?

A) The attendance on Friday has a greater median than attendance on Saturday, but both data sets have the same interquartile range.

B) The attendance on Friday has a greater interquartile range than attendance on Saturday, but both data sets have the same median.

C) The attendance on Friday has a greater median and a greater interquartile range than attendance on Saturday.
   The attendance on Friday and the attendance on Saturday have the same median and interquartile range.

SECTION 1 BASIC SKILLS

#	Answer	Topic	Subtopic	#	Answer	Topic	Subtopic	#	Answer	Topic	Subtopic	#	Answer	Topic	Subtopic
1	C	TA	S3	10	C	TA	S4	19	A	TA	S3	28	B	TA	S4
2	C	TA	S4	11	C	TA	S1	20	B	TA	S2	29	D	TA	S4
3	B	TA	S2	12	D	TA	S1	21	B	TA	S4	30	C	TA	S1
4	A	TA	S3	13	D	TA	S4	22	A	TA	S3	31	C	TA	S1
5	A	TA	S3	14	A	TA	S4	23	A	TA	S3	32	C	TA	S3
6	C	TA	S4	15	D	TA	S4	24	A	TA	S4	33	C	TA	S3
7	C	TA	S4	16	A	TA	S2	25	D	TA	S1	34	B	TA	S1
8	C	TA	S4	17	B	TA	S2	26	A	TA	S2	35	B	TA	S1
9	C	TA	S4	18	D	TA	S2	27	D	TA	S1	36	A	TA	S1

Topics & Subtopics

Code	Description	Code	Description
SA1	Basic Math	SA4	Language Skills
SA2	Logical Reasoning	TA	Basic Skills
SA3	Reading Comprehension		

13

CONTINUE ▶

TEST DIRECTION

DIRECTIONS

Read the questions carefully and then choose the ONE best answer to each question.

Be sure to allocate your time carefully so you are able to complete the entire test within the testing session. You may go back and review your answers at any time.

You may use any available space in your test booklet for scratch work.

Questions in this booklet are not actual test questions but they are the samples for commonly asked questions.

This test aims to cover all topics which may appear on the actual test. However some topics may not be covered.

Studying this booklet will be preparing you for the actual test. It will not guarantee improving your test score but it will help you pass your exam on the first attempt.

Some useful tips for answering multiple choice questions;

- Start with the questions that you can easily answer.

- Underline the keywords in the question.

- Be sure to read all the choices given.

- Watch for keywords such as NOT, always, only, all, never, completely.

- Do not forget to answer every question.

Answer the following six questions
according to this picture

At the Bank

1

As shown in the bank's wall clock, what can
we infer about the time of the day?

A) It is mid-afternoon.
B) It is lunchtime.
C) It is late afternoon.
D) It is early in the morning.

2

What is true about the woman in the
picture?

A) She is holding a pen.
B) She is wearing a pendant.
C) She is third in line.
D) She is carrying a handbag.

3

How do you describe the man wearing a hat?

A) He is talking to the customer behind
   him.
B) He is looking at his watch.
C) He is wearing a bow tie.
D) He is smoking a pipe.

4

What is true about the man who is wearing
sneakers?

A) He is looking at his notes.
B) He is writing notes.
C) He is speaking.
D) It cannot be told from this picture.

5

What is true about the man who is
reclining?

A) He is leaning on his left elbow
B) He is leaning on his right elbow.
C) He is writing.
D) He is raising one hand.

6

Which is true about the bank teller?

A) He is handing a change.
B) He is wearing glasses.
C) He is left-handed.
D) He is wearing a striped tie.

Answer the following four questions
according to this picture

The Meeting of The Board

7

How many people are there in the picture?

A) 7
B) 6
C) 5
D) 4

8

There are how many men wearing glasses?

A) 0
B) 1
C) 2
D) 4

9

Which of the following statements is
FALSE?

A) A total of seven men are on the table.
B) A map is posted behind the man sitting
   at the head of the table.
C) The man who is speaking is bald.
D) One of the men is looking at his watch.

10

What is true about the man at the head of
the table?

A) He is looking at a man on his right.
B) He is looking at the map.
C) He is reading his notes.
D) He is looking at a man on his left.

Refer to the following paragraph to answer the following three questions.

There is a need for creating and implementing a program that will protect our citizens and their property from criminal and antisocial acts, will effectively restrain and reform juvenile delinquents, and will prevent the further development of antisocial behavior. Law offenders must be given due discipline and punishment, and serious offenders must not be mollycoddled regardless of age under 21. Any antisocial acts should be subjected to restraints and punishment. It should be noted, however, that to make a punishment effective, it must be a planned part of a more comprehensive program of treating delinquency.

11

What does the preceding papragraph say about punishment?

A) Punishment is not effective to use with jevenile deliquents.
B) Punishment is the most effective means for reforming juvenile vandals and hooligans.
C) Punishment cannot be sufficiently used for serious offenders who are still minors.
D) Punishment needs to be a part of a complete program to make it effective in reducing juvenile delinquency.

12

Which of the following goals is not included in the preceding paragraph?

A) Treat juvenile delinquency and make youth offenders become useful citizens.
B) Stop the youth from demaging public property.
C) Organize an inter-city football league.
D) Protect homes from being broken into.

13

What does the preceding paragraph suggest about serious offenders who are under 21 years old?

A) They should be mollycoddled because they are minors.
B) They should be dealt with a program that punsihes mature criminals.
C) They should be punished.
D) They should be prevented by brute force.

14

Which of the following infractions earns the least severe punishment?

A) Misdemeanor
B) Felony
C) Violation
D) Crime

15

When equipment is properly passed from one officer to another

A) both officers are responsible.
B) the first officer using it is responsible
C) the last officer using it is responsible
D) no officer are responsible

16

Which of the following statements is true?

A) The last officer leaving an office must always close all the windows.
B) The last officer leaving an office must always turn off all the lights.
C) The last officer leaving an office does not have to always close the windows.
D) The last officer leaving an office must turn off all electrical devices.

17

In the U.S. government, what is the job of the Legislative Branch?

A) Implement laws
B) Make laws
C) Assess laws
D) Evaluate laws

18

During a presentation, which of the following phrases is appropriate for a formal greeting?

A) Let's get started
B) Listen up
C) Welcome
D) Be seated

19

Disciplinary detention, confining an inmate to a cell for 24 hour increments, is called as;

A) Holding cell
B) Solitary confinement
C) Cell confinement
D) Segregation

CONTINUE ▶

20

Which phrase about the jails is incorrect?

A) Rigidly for people who have been convicted of a felony
B) May or may not be for females
C) May or may not be for juveniles
D) Can hold more than the assigned number of people

21

Choose the best example of legal custody as it applies to the restraint of criminal?

A) Someone who has broken into a home is captured by a private citizen and now the person is being held until the authorities arrive.
B) A police officer made an unauthorized arrest and the person arrested is being brought to the station house.
C) An inmate is being transported to a hospital by a correction officer as a result of a court order.
D) A parent holds a youth who has broken a school window till school security staff arrive on the scene.

22

"An ideal correctional system should include several types of institutions to provide different degrees of custody."

What does the statement imply?

A) The degree of custody becomes stricter when there are a greater variety of institutions.
B) Different institutions in a correctional system offer different degrees of custody to its inmates.
C) The efficiency of the correctional system depends on the number of institutions it has.
D) The same type of correctional institution is not desirable for the custody of all prisoners.

23

Leading as a function of management involves a manager spending time connecting with his or her employees on an interpersonal level.

A commander chief tells his personal experience being in his first battle and the rate of successful missions to his worried troop members. Which of the following is the result of good leadership he demonstrated ?

A) Inspired followers
B) Initiated communication
C) Increased engagement
D) Shared knowledge

24

In which facilities are people convicted of terrorism usually incarcerated?

A) In death row of the state where the felons have committed acts of terror
B) In a federal prison, but the security level is determined on a case-by-case basis
C) Neither a nor b
D) Either a or b

25

Which of the following would be the best indication of high moral in a supervisor's unit?

A) The unit buys expensive birthday gifts for each other and their supervisor.
B) The unit never works overtime.
C) The supervisor often enjoys staying late to plan work for the following day.
D) The employees are willing to subordinate any personal desires they have to give first priority in attaining group objectives.

26

In criminal justice system, each department has different responsibilities. Which part of the criminal justice system is responsible for incarcerating convicted offenders?

A) Courts
B) Corrections
C) Police
D) Legislature

27

Which of the following statements regarding complaints is correct?

I. A complaint is an allegation of an improper or unlawful act committed by a correction officer provided that the act relates to the business of the correctional agency that employs the officer.
II. A complaint shall be thoroughly investigated by the supervisor to whom it was referred to and if the condition complained of exists, it shall be corrected and steps shall be taken to prevent its recurrence.
III. A complaint must be investigated by a supervisor.
IV. A complaint must involve an unlawful act

A) I and II
B) I, II and III
C) I, III and IV
D) I, II, III and IV

Team organizational design is where groups of employees are formed from various functional areas for the purpose of solving problems and exploring possibilities.

Which of the following is the importance in utilizing team organizational structure?

A) Increase competency among employees.
B) Create a more innovative approach by granting each department complete autonomy.
C) Break down functional barriers among departments to strengthen working relationships and improve efficiency.
D) Create a central department that will facilitate the decision making process

"The responsibilities of the housing authority includes settling every problem of private developers. The authority must conform to federal regulations and it must overcome the prejudices of contractors, bankets, and prospective tenant against public operations. The authority is also subjected to scrutinies for any errors in judgment or the first evident of high costs that can be torn to bits before a congressional committee."

Based on the selection, which statement would be most correct?

A) Housing authorities are no more immune to errors in judgment.
B) Contractors, bankers, and prospective tenants always support private builders' judgments.
C) A housing authority must deal with all the difficulties encountered by the private builder.
D) Investigations conducted by congressional committees impede the progress of public housing.

Which of the following actions must a supervisor take if one of his employees informs him that they feel like the supervisor is giving them much more work compared to other employees and that they are having trouble meeting the supervisor's deadlines?

A) Explain to the employee that he receives more work because is the most competent employee in the unit.
B) Determine if the employee is accurate by reviewing his recent assignments.
C) Inquire if the employee has been under a lot of work-related stress lately.
D) Explain that this is a busy time and that you are trying to divide the work equally within your unit.

Hierarchy is a way to structure an organization using different levels of authority and a vertical link, or chain of command, between superior and subordinate levels of the organization. In a hierarchical organization, which of the following is the best explanation of general communication?

A) There is no distinct flow of communication in a hierarchical organization.
B) Orders and information for decision making flow down the levels of the hierarchy.
C) Orders and information for decision making flow up the levels of the hierarchy.
D) Orders flow down and information for decision making flows up the levels of the hierarchy.

CONTINUE ▶

32

Which of the following would not be a good practice when you want to reprimand an employee for neglect of duty?

A) Have several days of cooling off period before dispensing the reprimand to your employee.

B) Only reprimand the employee in question when you are alone with them.

C) Present an opportunity for the employee to respond to your criticism.

D) When you are reprimanding the employee be sure to be very distinct about the particular act you are reprimanding them for.

SECTION 2 LIEUTENANT SKILLS

#	Answer	Topic	Subtopic	#	Answer	Topic	Subtopic	#	Answer	Topic	Subtopic	#	Answer	Topic	Subtopic
1	B	TB	S3	9	D	TB	S2	17	B	TB	S3	25	D	TB	S2
2	B	TB	S3	10	D	TB	S2	18	C	TB	S2	26	B	TB	S3
3	D	TB	S3	11	D	TB	S1	19	C	TB	S1	27	B	TB	S3
4	D	TB	S3	12	C	TB	S1	20	D	TB	S3	28	C	TB	S2
5	B	TB	S3	13	C	TB	S3	21	C	TB	S3	29	C	TB	S3
6	B	TB	S3	14	C	TB	S3	22	D	TB	S3	30	B	TB	S2
7	A	TB	S2	15	C	TB	S3	23	A	TB	S2	31	D	TB	S2
8	C	TB	S2	16	C	TB	S3	24	B	TB	S1	32	A	TB	S2

Topics & Subtopics

Code	Description	Code	Description
SB1	Detention Procedures	SB3	Career Specific Knowledge
SB2	Monitoring & Supervising Subordinates	TB	Lieutenant Skills

CONTINUE ▶

TEST DIRECTION

DIRECTIONS

Read the questions carefully and then choose the ONE best answer to each question.

Be sure to allocate your time carefully so you are able to complete the entire test within the testing session. You may go back and review your answers at any time.

You may use any available space in your test booklet for scratch work.

Questions in this booklet are not actual test questions but they are the samples for commonly asked questions.

This test aims to cover all topics which may appear on the actual test. However some topics may not be covered.

Studying this booklet will be preparing you for the actual test. It will not guarantee improving your test score but it will help you pass your exam on the first attempt.

Some useful tips for answering multiple choice questions;

- Start with the questions that you can easily answer.

- Underline the keywords in the question.

- Be sure to read all the choices given.

- Watch for keywords such as NOT, always, only, all, never, completely.

- Do not forget to answer every question.

CONTINUE ▶

1

You are given the following sentence. From the options below pick the most suitable words to accurately complete the sentence.

... cars can fit into ... parking spaces.

A) powerful; slow
B) compact; small
C) leased; borrowed
D) beautiful; expensive

2

You are given the following sentence. From the options below pick the most suitable words to accurately complete the sentence.

While most people simply walked by, some ... person stopped to ... the homeless man.

A) caring; annoy
B) kind; harass
C) considerate; help
D) dangerous; aid

3

"Five horses entered the stable, one at a time. Gold entered before Colors. Black entered before Colors, but after Champion. Thunder entered before Gold, but after Black."

What is the name of the horse who entered fourth?

A) Colors
B) Thunder
C) Gold
D) Black

4

You are given the following sentence. From the options below pick the most suitable words to accurately complete the sentence.

Robert's pants are very ... so he doesn't feel very ... in them.

A) tight; comfortable
B) large; tired
C) pretty; beautiful
D) long; short

26

CONTINUE ▶

5

"5 feet 11 inches is the height of the shortest member of the basketball team. Jaron is 6 feet 2 inches tall."

Which of the following is a fact when considering the passage above?

A) Jaron is shorter than some members of the basketball team.
B) At least one member of the basketball team is shorter than Jaron.
C) Only members of the basketball team are taller than 5 feet 11 inches.
D) Jaron is the tallest member of the basketball team.

6

Angel, a college student, claims that nitrogenous bases pair randomly with one another. Which of the following statements about nitrogenous base pairs opposes the student's stand?

A) "One member of a pair must be a purine and the other a pyrimidine in order to bridge between the two chains."
B) "The bases are joined together in pairs, a single base from one chain being hydrogen-bonded to a single base from the other."
C) "So far as is known, the sequence of bases along the chain is irregular."
D) "To each sugar is attached a nitrogenous base, which can be of four different types."

7

Lengths of Fish (in inches)						
9	7	10	11	8	10	11
11	12	12	12	12	13	13
14	14	15	15	15	16	25

The lengths of a random sample of 21 fish are listed in the table given above. The measurement of 25 inches is an error. Which of the mean, median, and range of the values listed above, will change the most if the 25 inch measurement is removed from the data?

A) Mean
B) Median
C) Range
D) All of them will change by the same amount.

8

You are given the following sentence. From the options below pick the most suitable words to accurately complete the sentence.

Attendance is not ... and employees are ... to arrive at the meeting at 16:00 o'clock.

A) questionable; instructed
B) necessary; needed
C) optional; required
D) expected; demanded

9

You are given the following sentence. From the options below pick the most suitable words to accurately complete the sentence.

The new cancer treatment has had a … impact, in spite of its … side effects.

A) serious; positive
B) beneficial; improving
C) serious; dangerous
D) positive; negative

10

You are given the following sentence. From the options below pick the most suitable words to accurately complete the sentence.

Unlike the … skin of a frog, that of a toad is much more textured and … .

A) green; brown
B) tough; scaly
C) slick; slimy
D) smooth; bumpy

11

The company _____ its employees to design a program that supports a clean and green _____.

A) incourages; environment
B) encourages; enviroment
C) encourages; environment
D) incourages; enviroment

12

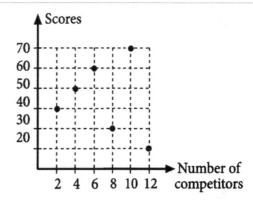

The scatter plot given above shows the sores of competitors in a performance competition. If the competitors who scored lower than 50 will be eliminated from the competition, how many competitors will be eliminated?

A) 8
B) 10
C) 20
D) 22

13

Which of the following sets of numbers is listed in ASCENDING order?

A) 5913, 5914, 5967, 5975, 5963, 5970, 5976
B) 5808, 5823, 5863, 5886, 5943, 5929, 5924
C) 5813, 5846, 5897, 5901, 5939, 5945, 5996
D) 5808, 5853, 5831, 5907, 5917, 5915, 5927

14

A prefix is a letter or group of letters that is added at the beginning of a word to change its meaning.

Which prefix means "opposite"?

A) re-
B) dis-
C) semi-
D) pre-

15

A suffix is a letter or group of letters that is added to the end of a word to change its meaning.

Which suffix means "more"?

A) -ful
B) -er
C) -ion
D) -est

16

"No man likes to acknowledge that he has made a mistake in the choice of his profession, and every man, worthy of the name, will row long against wind and tide before he allows himself to cry out, "I am baffled!" and submits to be floated passively back to land. From the first week of my residence in X — I felt my occupation irksome."

What is the main purpose of the passage as an opening sentence to an article?

A) It aims to contrast the narrator's good intentions with his malicious conduct.
B) It intends to establish the perspective of the narrator on a controversy.
C) It aims to offer a symbolic representation of the plight of Edward Crimsworth.
D) It intends to provide context which helps in understanding emotional state of the narrator.

CONTINUE ▶

17

"Part of this is about principles. Some will argue that space's "magnificent desolation" is not ours to despoil, just as they argue that our own planet's poles should remain pristine. Others will suggest that glutting ourselves on space's riches is not an acceptable alternative to developing more sustainable ways of earthly life.

History suggest that those will be hard lines to <u>hold</u>, and it may be difficult to persuade the public such barren environments are worth preserving."

In the passage above, the underline word is closely synonymous to which of the following?

A) grip
B) withstand
C) restrain
D) maintain

18

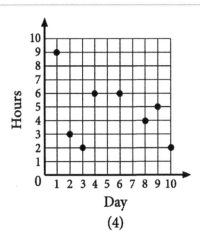

(4)

The scatterplot given above shows how many hours Eric worked for 10 days period. What is the average working hour for Eric for this 10 days period ?

A) 3.6
B) 3.7
C) 4.2
D) 4.6

CONTINUE ▶

19

"In the country of Genovia, all the painters are left-handed. Every Genovian painters is near-sighted."

Which of the following is fact with regards to the passage given?

A) At least some right-handed Genovians are painters.
B) At least some left-handed Genovians are near-sighted.
C) Every near-sighted Genovian is a teacher.
D) Every left-handed Cordovian is a teacher.

20

"Many flowering plants reproduce by means of pollination, a process that requires outside assistance."

Which of the following would most likely be the author mean in the passage?

A) The plants depends on pollinating agents such as water, wind, or flying creatures for pollination.
B) Mutations that are color-related are passed from parent to offspring.
C) Some ways of pollinations are intentional, while others are not.
D) Flowering plants are the only ones that can be reproduce via pollination.

21

"John Muir left home at an early age. He took a 1000-mile walk south to the Gulf of Mexco in 1867 and 1868. Then he sailed for San Francisco. The city was too noisy and crowded for Muir, so he headed inland for the Sierra Nevadas."

Consider the passage above. After John Muir arrived in San Francisco, what did he do?

A) During an earthquake, John Muir ran outside.
B) John Muir proposed a theory on how Yosemite was formed.
C) John Muir started to write articles regarding the Sierra Nevadas.
D) He traveled again towards the Sierra Nevadas.

22

At Lakewood School, each new student is paired with an older student partner. The new students are Baron, Georgia, Sanny, and Henry. The older student partners are Edward, Pau, Ryan, and Wilma. Sanny and Wilma are paired. Baron is not paired with Rhian. Edward is not paired with Georgia or Baron. Which of the following is true about the partner of Pau?

A) Pau is paired with Georgia.
B) Baron is the partner of Pau.
C) Pau is paired with Henry.
D) Edward is the partner of Pau.

23

The table below shows the numbers of gallons of gasoline used and the miles driven for different types of cars.

Gasoline Used and Miles Driven

Type of Car	Gallons of Gasoline Used	Miles Driven
A	4	140
B	8	220
C	16	320
D	20	400

Which type of car had the highest number of miles per gallon?

A) Type D
B) Type C
C) Type B
D) Type A

24

Three girls namely, Rhia, Therese and Xiera, each own one pet. The pets are a cockatoo, a rabbit and a guinea pig. Xiera does not own the guinea pig.

What additional piece of information is necessary to be able to determine who owns the rabbit?

A) Xiera owns the cockatoo.
B) Therese owns the guinea pig.
C) Rhia does not own the guinea pig.
D) Rhia owns the cockatoo.

25

How many pairs of numbers below are EXACTLY THE SAME?

545206581 – 545206581
275330968 – 275330968
892611899 – 892611894
147238117 – 147235117
821456849 – 821456849
651942565 – 651942565
972962749 – 972967249
350700517 – 350700517
497228991 – 497228991
213864748 – 213864748
655301147 – 655301147
980463326 – 980463362

A) eight pairs
B) nine pairs
C) ten pairs
D) eleven pairs

CONTINUE ▶

26

Read the following scenario and choose the best option from the list below.

Facts: In a Mark's family, everyone has a strict schedule. If Mark is late for school, his father will have to stay at work over schedule, and his mother will not serve dinner until his father is home. If Mark's mother does not serve dinner on time, Mark will snack on an apple. Mark's mother served dinner on time.

Conclusion: Mark was not late for school.

A) The facts neither prove nor disprove the conclusion.
B) The facts are in accordance with the conclusion.
C) The facts are not in accordance with the conclusion.
D) None of the above.

27

Johansen played three instruments in the orchestra. He played violin for two years, cello for three years, and bass for the three years. He never played more than two instruments during the same year. The first year, Johansen only played the violin.

What is the minimum number of years that Johansen could have played in the orchestra?

A) 7
B) 6
C) 5
D) 4

28

The table below represents the number of participants, y, on the Miami Middle School debate team after x years.

Debate Team

Year (x)	Number of Participants (y)
1	16
2	18
3	20
4	22
5	24

What is the relationship between the number of participants on the debate team and the year?

A) $y = x + 16$
B) $y = 2x + 16$
C) $y = 16x + 2$
D) $y = 2x + 14$

Ryan read 9 books over the summer. He recorded the number of pages he read and the number of hours he spent reading each book. This information and a line of best fit are shown in the scatter plot.

Books Ryan Read

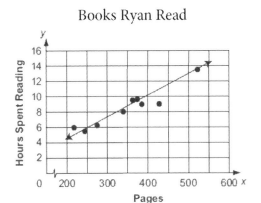

Based on the scatter plot, which statement about the time Ryan spent reading would most likely be true?

A) It would take Ryan about 12 hours to read a 470-page book.

B) Ryan read at a rate of about 50 pages per hour.

C) Ryan read at a rate of about 75 pages per hour.

D) It would take Ryan about 2 hours to read a 150-page book.

- "It takes two to make a quarrel," Marco instructed her.

"I guess it only takes one to act like an idiot," his sister replied. "Stop it!"

"Familiarity breeds contempt," said Marco sadly. "Let's forgive and forget." -

The passage above is taken from the "A Word in the Hand". On the last part of the dialogue, what does the word "contempt" mean?

A) doubt

B) emotion

C) dislike

D) anxiety

"Human beings have only one stomach, one heart, and one brain… right? Not exactly. The cerebral cortex, the most advanced part of the brain, might be thought as two structures, connected by a band of fibers called the corpus callosum. Each structure, or hemisphere, performs different tasks and is responsible for different functions."

Based on this passage, which of the following is the most appropriate illustration of the function of the corpus callosum?

A) It is like a computer disk used to store condensed information.
B) It is like a spark plug designed to ignite the fuel in a combustion engine.
C) It is like a fiber-optic cable used to connect telephone networks.
D) It is like a satellite dish designed to receive directed signals.

"Before you can choose a password, however, you must know the types of passwords required. First find out if all letters must be lowercase or if upper- and lowercase are both acceptable. Should the password consist of letters or numbers only, or are special characters permissible? What is the minimum and maximum length allowed?"

Based on the passage given, before a person chooses a password, what should be done?

A) One should think of something unforgettable from the past.
B) One should decide where to store the information to keep it safe.
C) One should determine what type of password must be used.
D) One should change your password about every three months.

33

"In addition to making these investigations, archaeologists have been able to stud the skeletons of victims by using distilled water to wash away the volcanic ash. By strengthening the brittle bone with acrylic paint, scientists have been able to examine the skeletons and draw conclusions about the diet and habits of the residents."

In the given passage, what does the word "distilled" mean?

A) sea
B) volcanic
C) bottled
D) purified

34

"The Human Resources Packet will include information about the Gorman Productions Web site, other helpful Web sites, computer information, a sample production schedule, and security statement. You are responsible for familiarizing yourself with this information before your first day of work in the production studio. In this same packet, you will also find a New Team Member Orientation Evaluation Survey."

According to the passage above, which of the following materials is included in the Human Resources Packet?

A) The supervisor's schedule
B) A payroll form
C) A Photo ID badge
D) The security statement

35

"Jacob has three pets at home: a hedgehog, which is only active only at night; a dog, which is only active during the day; and a cat, which alternately sleeps for an hour and then active for an hour."

Which of the following must be true about the activity of Jacob's pets?

A) The cat and the dog will never be active simultaneously.
B) The cat and the hedgehog will never be active simultaneously.
C) There will never be more than two pets that are active simultaneously.
D) At alternate hours, all three animals are active.

"John Muir was born in 1838 in Scotland. His family name means "moor", which is a meador full or flowers and animals. John loved nature from the time he was small. He also liked to climb rocky cliffs and walls.

When John was 11 years old, his family moved to the United States and settled in Wisconsin. John was good with tools and soon became an inventor. He first invented a model of a sawmill. Later, he invented an alarm clock that would cause the sleeping person to be tipped out of the bed when the timer sounded."

Based from the passage above, when did John Muir invented an alarm clock?

A) While John Muir and his family lived in Wisconsin.
B) While John Muir and his famiy was still living in Scotland.
C) After John Muir took a trip in Yosemite
D) After John Muir traveled to San Francisco.

SECTION 3 BASIC SKILLS

#	Answer	Topic	Subtopic	#	Answer	Topic	Subtopic	#	Answer	Topic	Subtopic	#	Answer	Topic	Subtopic
1	B	TA	S4	10	D	TA	S4	19	B	TA	S3	28	D	TA	S1
2	C	TA	S4	11	C	TA	S4	20	A	TA	S3	29	A	TA	S1
3	C	TA	S3	12	D	TA	S1	21	D	TA	S3	30	C	TA	S4
4	A	TA	S4	13	C	TA	S1	22	B	TA	S3	31	C	TA	S3
5	B	TA	S3	14	B	TA	S4	23	D	TA	S1	32	C	TA	S3
6	A	TA	S3	15	B	TA	S4	24	D	TA	S3	33	D	TA	S3
7	C	TA	S1	16	D	TA	S3	25	A	TA	S1	34	D	TA	S3
8	C	TA	S4	17	D	TA	S3	26	C	TA	S2	35	C	TA	S3
9	D	TA	S4	18	B	TA	S1	27	C	TA	S3	36	B	TA	S4

Topics & Subtopics

Code	Description	Code	Description
SA1	Basic Math	SA4	Language Skills
SA2	Logical Reasoning	TA	Basic Skills
SA3	Reading Comprehension		

CONTINUE ▶

TEST DIRECTION

DIRECTIONS

Read the questions carefully and then choose the ONE best answer to each question.

Be sure to allocate your time carefully so you are able to complete the entire test within the testing session. You may go back and review your answers at any time.

You may use any available space in your test booklet for scratch work.

Questions in this booklet are not actual test questions but they are the samples for commonly asked questions.

This test aims to cover all topics which may appear on the actual test. However some topics may not be covered.

Studying this booklet will be preparing you for the actual test. It will not guarantee improving your test score but it will help you pass your exam on the first attempt.

Some useful tips for answering multiple choice questions;

- Start with the questions that you can easily answer.

- Underline the keywords in the question.

- Be sure to read all the choices given.

- Watch for keywords such as NOT, always, only, all, never, completely.

- Do not forget to answer every question.

CONTINUE ▶

Refer to the following paragraph to answer the following two questions.

There are different types of inmates, namely: gorillas, toughs, hipsters, and merchants. The gorillas deliberately use violence to bring fear to inmates and exploit them into providing favor. The toughs are violence-seekers against prisoners who insult them, but they do not exploit others. The hipsters are bullies who choose victims with caution. They demonstrate false physical bravery to win acceptance among inmates. The merchants exploit other inmates through overpriced trading of goods stolen from prison supplies.

1

George and Gregory are fearful to Brooks because the latter frequently beats them both. Thus, George and Gregory give cigarettes and money to Brooks because of fear for him.

Based on the situation, what type of inmate is Brooks?

A) hipster
B) gorilla
C) tough
D) merchant

2

Johnson and Stevenson are often scheduled for the same cleaning duty and exercise group. Johnson is cross-eyed, and it often appears that he is directing his gaze in one direction. One day, Stevenson beats Johnson because he felt insulted on the way the latter stares at him.

Based on the situation, Stevenson can be classified as a

A) tough
B) hipster
C) merchant
D) gorilla

Refer to the following paragraphs to answer the following ten questions.

Burglary refers to the act in which a person enters a building to commit a crime therein.

Larceny refers to the act in which a person wrongfully takes, obtains, or withholds the property of another.

Robbery refers to the act of forcible stealing of property. If larceny involves threatening to the victim, the crime changes to robbery.

Sexual abuse refers to the act in which a person subjects another person to sexual contact without the latter's consent, or when a person has sexual contact with somebody who is less than 17 years of age. "Sexual contact" may be defined as touching the sexual or other intimate parts of a person to achieve sexual gratification.

Sexual misconduct refers to the act in which a male has sexual intercourse with a consenting female who is at least 13 years old but less than 17 years old.

Harassment refers to the act in which a person intends to harass, annoy, or alarm another person through striking, shoving, kicking, or otherwise subjecting the other person to physical contact.

Assault refers to the act in which a person unlawfully causes a physical injury to another person.

3

Stephen Smith invited his 17-year-old girlfriend to go to his apartment to have a sexual intercourse with him. His girlfriend agreed.

Based on the situation, Smith could be charged with

A) sexual misconduct
B) sexual abuse
C) both sexual misconduct and burglary
D) no crime, as her girlfriend consented to the activity

CONTINUE ▶

4

Ben Dawson attends a crowded party. After a while, he notices a woman, dressed in miniskirt and sleeveless, who is busy talking with her friends. Dawson approaches the woman, and without saying anything, touches her butt. The woman is astounded, and moves away from him. As she does, Dawson slips her iPhone in his pocket and walks away.

Which is certain to be charged with Dawson?

A) sexual misconduct, burglary, and larceny
B) sexual misconduct, robbery, and larceny
C) sexual abuse, burglary and robbery
D) sexual abuse and larceny

5

During one of her campaign speeches, Mary heard James, an opposition supporter, making a derogatory comment about her. After her speech, Mary confronted James to make an apology, but he refused. Mary slapped him out of anger, and immediately walked away.

Based on the situation, Mary could be charged with

A) sexual misconduct and assault
B) burglary and harassment
C) harassment
D) assault

6

Ryan had a quarrel with his wife before leaving for work. On his way to his office, he encountered a traffic incident which enraged his bad mood farther. As he was about to make a negotiation with the other vehicle's owner, the latter made a cursing remark. This made Ryan grew angrier, causing him to punch the man twice on his face.

Based on the situation, Ryan could be chraged with

A) assault
B) harassment
C) harassment and assault
D) no crime was committed, as the man caused Ryan to be emotionally upset

7

John David, 24 years old, had a sexual intercourse with his 16-year-old girlfriend in her apartment, with her consent.

Based on the situation, David could be charged with

A) sexual misconduct
B) both burglary and sexual abuse
C) both burglary and sexual misconduct
D) no crime, as his girlfriend consented to the activity

8

Tim Sawyer entered into the condominium unit of his female colleague with the intent to sexually abuse her. Fortunately, his colleague left home for a party before he came. Thus, Sawyer left the condominium in frustration.

Based on the situation, Sawyer could be charged with

A) sexual misconduct
B) sexual abuse
C) burglary
D) No crime was committed, as Sawyer was not able to do his intention

9

Martin Piery enters a home with the intention of taking the computer set in the living room. The home owner fortunately wakes up, and attempts to retrieve the computer set from Piery. To get out safely, Piery kicks the home owner and runs out immediately.

Based on the situation, Piery can be charged with

A) burglary only
B) burglary and larceny
C) robbery and larceny
D) burglary and robbery

10

George Stevens enters a department store to shop some groceries. Upon passing the gadgets counter, he notices the latest iphone model in the display shelf. After checking the surrounding and knowing that nobody is observing him, he slips the iphone in his pocket and immediately leaves the store.

Based on the situation, Stevens can be charged with

A) larceny
B) robbery
C) burglary and robbery
D) burglary and larceny

11

Brandon enters a gadget store through its back window at 3:00 a.m. He takes two laptop sets and three mobile phones. As he is about to leave, a security guard noticed him. He attempts to run, but the guard grabs his left hand. He thus kicks the guard on his buttocks which makes him become unconscious instantly. Brandon then immediately runs away from the store.

Based on the situation, Brandon could be charged with

A) robbery, larceny, and assault
B) burglary, larceny, and assault
C) burglary, larceny, and robbery
D) burglary, robbery, and assault

12

Kate and Tim are partners in a college biology research project. One afternoon after class, Kaye invites Tim to come to her house to do some research. They are in Kate's room, when Tim feels the urge to have sex with Kate. Kate attempts to stop him, but Tim proceeds to caress her breasts and touch her private parts. Kate screams for help, which caused Tim to rush away from the house.

Based on the situation, Tim could be charged with

A) burglary and sexual misconduct
B) burglary and sexual abuse
C) sexual abuse
D) no crime, as Kate invited Tim to her house

13

A person can support an inmate by sending money or packages. This person is called as;

A) Representative
B) Runner
C) Smuggler
D) Felon

14

Reports are effective if they are descriptive enough. Which of the following sentences in a report is the most descriptive?

A) The behaviors of inmate X was hostile.
B) When I talked to Inmate Y she wasn't acting cooperatively.
C) Inmate Z indicated that she would not submit to custody.
D) Inmate T said, "You can not send me to the laundry"

15

Communication is sending and receiving information between two or more people. The person sending the message is referred to as the sender, while the person receiving the information is called the receiver. During a communication, which of the following type of information is not usually conveyed?

A) Attitudes
B) Emotions
C) Private thoughts
D) Beliefs

16

Which phrase is incorrect about prisons?

A) Prisons can have a death row, depending on approved organization and layout
B) Prisons are applicable to both state and federal incarceration facilities
C) Prisons should not be for female inmates, regardless of age or physical strength
D) Prisons are technically only for convicted felons

17

Which of the following statements is true?

A) A crime is always a felony.
B) A crime is always a misdemeanor.
C) A crime is either a violation or a misdemeanor.
D) A crime is either a felony or a misdemeanor.

18

Decision making involves the selection of a course of action from among two or more possible alternatives in order to arrive at a solution for a given problem. Which of the following is the impact on individual's decision-making when working for a large organization?

A) They have more hands-on activities.
B) They have less input in decision-making.
C) They should consider anyone's welfare.
D) They are charged with making strategic decisions.

19

Statement 1: A correction officer should conduct a filed search of a prisoner to check for evidence, weapons, and other contraband.
Statement 2: A prisoner arrested by a correction officer must always be given Miranda Rights.

Which of the following choices is most accurate in describing the two statements given above?

A) Only statement 1 is correct.
B) Only statement 2 is correct.
C) Neither statement 1 nor 2 is correct.
D) Both statements 1 and 2 are correct.

Sexual harassment is unwanted sexual advances, obscene remarks or any other offensive sexually motivated material or communication. A company's secretary believes that she has been a victim of a sexual harrassment. Which of the following step should she do next?

A) She should leave the company.
B) She should take revenge on the person who sexually harassed her.
C) She should schedule a meeting to speak to HR.
D) She should simply ignore the behavior and hope it stops.

## 21

"Unemployment of young men from minority groups often causes them to become discouraged and hopeless economically, causing them to resort to any means of supplying their wants."

Based on the paragraph, we can infer that

A) discouragement sometimes leads to crime
B) unemployment turns young men from crime
C) most young men from minority groups are criminals
D) young men from minority groups are mostly unemployed

## 22

A leader's role in an organization can be formally assigned by his or her position, like manager or department head, and it can also be informally assumed by an employee who possesses a certain charisma that attracts others to follow. Which of the following is the difference of unassigned and assigned leadership roles?

A) Motivating employees is more important in assigned leadership roles.
B) Personality traits are more important in unassigned leadership roles
C) Organizing and directing people to perform tasks is more important in unassigned leadership roles.
D) Charismatic influence is more important in assigned leadership roles.

"To prevent crime, our aim should be not merely to reform the law breakers but to strike at the roots of crime parents, bad companions, unsatisfactory homes, selfishness, disregard for the rights of others, and bad social conditions."

Based on the statement, there is a need to

A) impose compulsory education
B) create better reformatories
C) abolish prisons
D) create general social reform

24

Placement of an inmate in a controlled unit for the safety and security of the institution is regarded as:

A) Administrative segregation.
B) Inmate segregation.
C) One-on-one observation.
D) Punishment.

25

U.S. Equal Employment Opportunity Commission, or EEOC is responsible for enforcing the laws that make it illegal to discriminate against a job applicant.

Which of the following does not include in the EEOC category for anti-discrimination?

A) Religion
B) National origin
C) Age
D) Actions

26

Which of the following disciplinary sanction for erring inmates is not allowed?

A) Prohibiting some activities
B) Restraining some devices
C) Segregating from other inmates
D) Withholding of some privileges

27

Controlling is the final function of management. Once a plan has been carried out, the manager evaluates the results against the goals.

A company manager adjusted his team sales goal after reviewing each performance record to allow additional quality control measures since their production goals for the past four months decline. Which of the following makes the manager controlling?

A) Manager looked at team results and took appropriate corrective action.
B) Manager acted as a leader and took responsibility for the project.
C) Manager is overseeing his employess.
D) Manager is analyzing if there is a need to cut off the number of employees.

Herzberg developed a theory of workplace motivation called the two-factor theory. The two-factor theory is based on the assumption that there are two sets of factors that influence motivation in the workplace by either enhancing employee satisfaction or hindering it.

Which of the following can employee dissatisfaction be eliminated according to Herzberg?

A) By finding the right balance between hygiene factors and motivators
B) By remedying the causes of dissatisfaction
C) By giving another task to be done
D) By lessening workload to each employee

SECTION 4 LIEUTENANT SKILLS

#	Answer	Topic	Subtopic	#	Answer	Topic	Subtopic	#	Answer	Topic	Subtopic	#	Answer	Topic	Subtopic
1	B	TB	S2	8	C	TB	S1	15	C	TB	S2	22	B	TB	S2
2	A	TB	S3	9	D	TB	S1	16	C	TB	S3	23	D	TB	S3
3	D	TB	S1	10	A	TB	S1	17	D	TB	S3	24	A	TB	S1
4	D	TB	S1	11	D	TB	S1	18	B	TB	S2	25	D	TB	S2
5	C	TB	S1	12	C	TB	S3	19	A	TB	S1	26	B	TB	S3
6	A	TB	S1	13	B	TB	S3	20	C	TB	S2	27	A	TB	S2
7	C	TB	S1	14	D	TB	S3	21	A	TB	S3	28	A	TB	S2

Topics & Subtopics

Code	Description	Code	Description
SB1	Detention Procedures	SB3	Career Specific Knowledge
SB2	Monitoring & Supervising Subordinates	TB	Lieutenant Skills

TEST DIRECTION

DIRECTIONS

Read the questions carefully and then choose the ONE best answer to each question.

Be sure to allocate your time carefully so you are able to complete the entire test within the testing session. You may go back and review your answers at any time.

You may use any available space in your test booklet for scratch work.

Questions in this booklet are not actual test questions but they are the samples for commonly asked questions.

This test aims to cover all topics which may appear on the actual test. However some topics may not be covered.

Studying this booklet will be preparing you for the actual test. It will not guarantee improving your test score but it will help you pass your exam on the first attempt.

Some useful tips for answering multiple choice questions;

- Start with the questions that you can easily answer.

- Underline the keywords in the question.

- Be sure to read all the choices given.

- Watch for keywords such as NOT, always, only, all, never, completely.

- Do not forget to answer every question.

CONTINUE ▶

1

You are given the following sentence. From the options below pick the most suitable words to accurately complete the sentence.

In spite of her advanced ... , his childish behavior made Sean appear ... .

A) manners; polite
B) brightness; dull
C) appearance; shy
D) age; immature

2

Implementing a _____ program has many considerations that _____ crucial to its success.

A) mentoring; are
B) mentering; are
C) mentoring; is
D) mentering; is

3

All team leaders are required to _____ in the conference room, _____ present their project proposals.

A) proceed; than
B) precede; than
C) precede, then
D) proceed; then

4

A successful organization maintains _____ among _____ members.

A) consensus; its
B) concensus; its
C) consensus; it's
D) concensus; it's

5

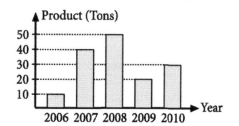

A companies production capacity is given in the above column chart. In which years company produced below its average capacity ?

A) 2006 and 2010
B) 2006 and 2009
C) 2009 and 2010
D) 2006 and 2007

6

You are given the following sentence. From the options below pick the most suitable words to accurately complete the sentence.

I did ... on the test because I ... very hard.

A) quickly; ran
B) poorly; worked
C) badly; prepared
D) well; studied

CONTINUE ▶

7

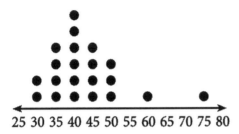

25 30 35 40 45 50 55 60 65 70 75 80
Average Flight delay (in minutes)

The average delay of flights for each of the largest 21 airline companies in Asia, was calculated and shown in the dot plot above. If the highest flight delay is removed from the dot plot, which of the following changes ocur?

A) The average will decrease only.
B) The average and median will decrease only.
C) The range and average will decrease only.
D) The median, range, and average will decrease.

8

"If it is snowing, John can't ride his bike. If it is dark, John can't ride his bike."

Which of the following sentences is a fact based on the passage above?

A) If John can't ride his bike, then it must be snowing.
B) If John rides his bikes, then it is not dark or snowing.
C) If John can't ride his bike, then it must be dark.
D) John don't have a headlight on his bike.

9

You are given the following number. How many digits appear more than three times?

3290129875010938479817907077546789

A) 4
B) 5
C) 6
D) None of the above

10

"The researchers were also able to devise a mathematical model that describes the movement and formation of these waves."

What does the word "devise" mean in the passage?

A) start
B) solve
C) imagine
D) create

11

You are given the following sentence. From the options below pick the most suitable words to accurately complete the sentence.

The leftover pizza in the fridge smelled rotten, yet I … decided to … it.

A) quickly; ingest
B) warily; throw
C) foolishly; consume
D) wisely; eat

12

The results of a survey in which college students were asked how many meals they typically eat per day is given by the graph below.

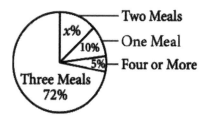

If 1200 students responded to the survey, how many of them reported that they typically eat two meals per day?

A) 60
B) 120
C) 156
D) 180

13

How long does it take to drive a certain route if the driver starts at 9:50 A.M. to 2:05 P.M. to complete the said route?

A) 4 hours and 15 minutes
B) 4 hours and 35 minutes
C) 5 hours and 15 minutes
D) 6 hours and 25 minutes

14

"Significant statistical evidence shows that more people die due to heart diseases than any other illnesses. People who are over 30 years of age are more prone to developing heart diseases, with a 50-50 chance of acquiring the disease. Due to the population explosion for the past years, more and more people are being diagnosed with heart diseases."

Based on the paragraph, what is most correct to say about heart disease?

A) The increasing possibility of dying due to a heart disease is caused by the increasing population.
B) Half of the population who are at least 30 years old have heart disease today.
C) Older people are the chief victims of heart disease.
D) More people die of heart disease than all of the other diseases combined.

If atoms are the letters of the chemical language, then molecules are the words. But in order to put the chemical letters together to form chemical words, we have to know something about the rules of chemical spelling.

The discussion of atoms is introduced in the passage above by using which technique?

A) An analogy
B) An aphorism
C) An example
D) A hypothesis

You are given the following scenario, choose the best option from the list below.

Facts: A group of friends are trying to decide how to spend their afternoon. If John goes to see a movie, Anna will accompany him. But if this happens, she will be tired the next day. Dean will only go to the movies if Roland goes too. Roland will only go to the movies if John goes too. Dean ended up not going to the movies.

Conclusion: Anna was tired the following day.

A) The facts neither prove nor disprove the conclusion.
B) The facts are in accordance with the conclusion.
C) The facts are not in accordance with the conclusion.
D) None of the above.

You are given the following scenario, choose the best option from the list below.

Facts: Andrea, Bee, Charlie and Sharon all sat their Maths exam. Charlie received the lowest grade. Andrea did not get the highest grade. Bee got a 93 while Sharon got a 77. The mean average grade was 82. No two students had the same grade.

Conclusion: Andrea's grade was not below the mean average grade.

A) The facts neither prove nor disprove the conclusion.
B) The facts are in accordance with the conclusion.
C) The facts are not in accordance with the conclusion.
D) None of the above.

Read the following scenario and choose the best option from the list below.

Facts: Catherine has a very active lifestyle and tries to keep in shape by jogging around the neighborhood every morning unless the weather is bad, and it's snowing or raining. When this happens she uses the treadmill she has installed in the basement. On Tuesday, Catherine jogged outside.

Conclusion: The weather was not bad on Tuesday, therefore it did not rain or snow.

A) The facts neither prove nor disprove the conclusion.
B) The facts are not in accordance with the conclusion.
C) The facts are in accordance with the conclusion.
D) None of the above.

19

You are given the following scenario, choose the best option from the list below.

Facts: Four friends deliver fliers for a company and are paid according to how many fliers they distribute. Gary receives $40, while Chloe receives more than Daisy, but less than twice as much as Gary, and Arthur receives $60 more than Chloe.

Conclusion: Chloe delivers more fliers than Gary.

A) The facts neither prove nor disprove the conclusion.
B) The facts are in accordance with the conclusion.
C) The facts are not in accordance with the conclusion.
D) None of the above.

20

Given the following scenario, choose the best option from the list below.

Facts: Jane is 20 years old. She is twice as old as John, who is 5 years older than Matt.

Conclusion: John is 40 years old.

A) The facts neither prove nor disprove the conclusion.
B) The facts are in accordance with the conclusion.
C) The facts are not in accordance with the conclusion.
D) None of the above.

21

Omega 3 Content per 100 g	
X_1	0.12 mg
X_2	0.10 mg
X_3	11.44 mg
X_4	0.02 mg
X_5	9.09 mg

The data in the table above shows the average Omega 3 content per 100 grams of fish oil. Which of the following is closest to the expected amount of X_3 in 20 grams of fish oil?

A) 0.024 mg
B) 0.02 mg
C) 1.818 mg
D) 2.288 mg

22

You are given the following sentence. From the options below pick the most suitable words to accurately complete the sentence.

The audience at the performance was ... and the actors were repeatedly ... .

A) supportive; applauded
B) gracious; criticized
C) happy; ignored
D) helpful; praised

23

"All of Sam's friends who are in the senior class voted for her for president of the school council. Some of Sam's friends voted for Tony for president of the school council.

Which of the following is a fact regarding the given passage?

A) Sam has friends who are not in the senior class.
B) If Noemi is not Sam's friend, then he voted for Tony.
C) If Yani is Sam's friend, then she voted for Sam.
D) All of Sam's friends are in the senior class.

24

Consider the passage from the article "Electric Cars Deserve Second Look":

"Furthermore, the federal government is encouraging electric car use by giving significant rebates for purchasing electric cars, and some offer additional rebates."

Which of the following is the meaning of the word rebate in the given passage?

A) awards
B) additional guarantees
C) tax credits
D) money returned

25

"Although the blossoms of most wild plants are still green or white, there are more colors now than there were 150 million years ago. Of these newer colors, yellow shades are the most common, followed by orange and red, including shades of pink. Blue flowers are the rarest, because relatively few mutations resulted in that color."

Based on the passage, why are blue flowers so rare?

A) Blue flowers are avoided by bees and other insects.
B) Bees can't see the color blue
C) Blue flowers don't have carotene.
D) Only few mutations results in blue color.

"A one-room school has three grades—6th, 7th, and 8th. There are eight students attending the school: Alex, Ben, Carrie, Donna, Eddy, Fia, Greg and Hana. In each grade there are either two or three students. Alex, Donna and Fia are all in different grades. Ben and Eddy are both in the 7th grade, and Hana and Carrie are in the same grade."

Which of the following must be true considering the given passage?

A) Three students are in the 7th grade, exactly.

B) Two students are in the 6th grade, exactly.

C) Carrie and Donna are in the same grade.

D) Fia is in the 8th grade.

## 27

"Anthropologists describe gift-giving as a positive social process, serving various political, religious and psychological functions. Economists, however, offer a less favorable view. According to Waldfogel (1993), gift-giving represents an objective waste of resources. People buy gifts that recipients would not choose to buy on their own, or at least not spend as much money to purchase) a phenomenon (referred to as "the deadweight loss of Christmas"). To wit, givers are likely to spend $100 to purchase a gift that receivers would spend only $80 to buy themselves. This "deadweight loss" suggests that gift-givers are not very good at predicting what gifts others will appreciate. That in itself is not surprising to social psychologists. Research has found that people often struggle to take account of others' perspectives—their insights are subject to egocentrism, social projection, and multiple attribution errors."

Consider the passage above. What is the most appropriate description for the "deadweight loss" phenomenon mentioned by social psychologists in the passage?

A) Questionable

B) Predictable

C) Unprecedented

D) Disturbing

28

"Your essay must be at least 1,000 words, but no longer than 1,500 words. All entries that do not meet this length requirement will be automatically disqualified. Be certain that your area is rich with historical facts. Mark each fact as an endnote. Include a full biography with your entry. Points will be subtracted for weak grammar and poor spelling. While we prefer typed entries, handwritten entries are allowed, but we must be able to read your handwriting."

Based on the rules in the given passage, which of the essays would be subjected to disqualification?

A) an essay that is handwritten
B) an essay with 1,600 words
C) an essay with uninteresting facts
D) an essay about Rainbow Cliffes

SECTION 5 BASIC SKILLS

#	Answer	Topic	Subtopic	#	Answer	Topic	Subtopic	#	Answer	Topic	Subtopic	#	Answer	Topic	Subtopic
1	D	TA	S4	8	B	TA	S3	15	A	TA	S1	22	A	TA	S4
2	A	TA	S4	9	C	TA	S1	16	B	TA	S2	23	A	TA	S3
3	D	TA	S4	10	D	TA	S3	17	B	TA	S2	24	A	TA	S3
4	A	TA	S4	11	C	TA	S4	18	C	TA	S2	25	D	TA	S3
5	B	TA	S1	12	C	TA	S1	19	A	TA	S2	26	A	TA	S3
6	D	TA	S4	13	A	TA	S1	20	C	TA	S2	27	B	TA	S3
7	C	TA	S1	14	C	TA	S3	21	D	TA	S1	28	B	TA	S3

Topics & Subtopics

Code	Description	Code	Description
SA1	Basic Math	SA4	Language Skills
SA2	Logical Reasoning	TA	Basic Skills
SA3	Reading Comprehension		

CONTINUE ▶

Made in the USA
Las Vegas, NV
23 October 2024